FAMOUS PEOPLE

Biographies of
support the curriculum.

Helen Keller

by Harriet Castor
Illustrations by Nick Ward

W

FRANKLIN WATTS
LONDON•SYDNEY

First Published in 1998
by Franklin Watts
This edition 2001

Franklin Watts
96 Leonard Street
London EC2A 4XD

Franklin Watts Australia
56 O'Riordan Street
Alexandria, Sydney
NSW 2015

ISBN 0 7496 4311 0

A CIP catalogue record for this book is
available from the British Library

Dewey Decimal Classification
Number: 362 4

10 9 8 7 6 5 4 3 2 1

Series Editor: Sarah Ridley
Designer: Kirstie Billingham
Consultant: Dr. Anne Millard

Printed in Great Britain

Helen Keller

Helen Keller was born in 1880, in Alabama in the USA. For eighteen months she was a bright, happy, healthy baby. But then she developed a strange illness.

Helen got better, but
the illness left her deaf
and blind. Her world
had become silent
and dark.

Helen's parents took her to see many doctors, but none of them could help. Helen could not go to school. She could not learn to talk or read.

Instead, Helen made up lots of signs to tell people what she wanted. But if they refused her, or didn't understand, she often became so frustrated that she flew into a rage.

That's her sign for 'mother'.

Some of Helen's relatives
thought she had a mental
disability and should be sent
away to a special home.

Helen's mother heard about a school where another deaf-blind girl had been taught. She asked the school to send a teacher for Helen. When Helen was six, Annie Sullivan arrived.

Annie had had a sad childhood and had trouble with her sight, too. But she was strong-willed and lively.

9

Straight away, Annie began to spell words into Helen's hand. She made a sign for each letter with her fingers. She had brought Helen a doll as a present. So she spelt out D-O-L-L.

Helen imitated the hand signs, but did not know what they meant.

Annie wanted Helen to behave
well. At meals Helen grabbed
food from other people's plates.
Annie made her eat from her own
plate and use a spoon, though
Helen kicked and screamed.

In one lesson, Helen knocked out two of Annie's teeth – but Annie wasn't put off!

Helen's parents hated to see
Helen upset. So Annie
persuaded them to let her move
with Helen to a little garden
house nearby.

Helen was taken for a long walk on the way there and Annie rearranged the furniture inside, so Helen wouldn't know where she was.

15

When Helen became more obedient, she and Annie moved back home. Helen had learnt lots of words, but still didn't know what they were for.

Then one day, Annie put Helen's hand under the water pump and spelled 'water' over and over. Suddenly Helen realised that 'water' was the name for what she could feel.

She understands! It's a miracle!

Helen was thrilled, and asked Annie the name of everything around her. She had a very good memory and learnt lots of new words every day.

Helen no longer fought against Annie. She quickly came to love 'Teacher' dearly, and they laughed and played together.

Annie realised that Helen would
be her life's work. She read a
great deal about how to teach
deaf-blind children, but in the
end made up her own way of
doing it. It worked brilliantly.

It was exhausting, though. Helen
wanted to spell to Annie all day.
If Annie refused, Helen spelt into
her own hand.

After only four months, Helen wrote her first letter. Her paper was fitted over a board with grooves in it, to help guide her pencil.

Helen will write mother
letter papa did give hel-
en medicine mildred
will sit in swing
mildred will kiss
helen teacher did give
helen peach
jimmie is sick in
bed george on mishunt
anna did give helen
lemonade do

Helen also learnt Braille. This is
a system of raised dots that lets
you read by touch.

Helen loved lessons so much she had to be persuaded to rest! Annie took her on long walks — but Helen asked so many questions that these were like lessons, too.

When Helen was nine, she decided to learn to speak.

Annie took her to a special teacher. Helen put one hand on the teacher's face and the other in her mouth. Soon, she was saying words herself.

Helen worked on her speech for many years. People who didn't know her, though, often found her difficult to understand.

Helen quickly became famous. She used her fame to help other deaf-blind children. When she was eleven, she decided to hold a fund-raising tea party. It was very successful.

Soon, Helen began writing for magazines. She decided to be a writer when she grew up.

29

Helen still worked very hard at her studies. It was unusual for women to go to university then, but she won a place at Radcliffe – a women's college attached to the famous Harvard University. In the difficult English entrance exam, Helen did better than any other student, male or female.

Annie went to Radcliffe with Helen. She spelt every lecture into Helen's hand, and often had to spell whole books too, when there were no copies in Braille.

It was very tiring. But Annie
was determined Helen should
do well. Helen worked hard and
got her degree.

After Radcliffe, Helen and Annie wrote books and articles, gave lectures and raised money for the deaf-blind.

They toured all around the USA, and later travelled abroad too. Over the years Helen visited many countries, including South Africa, Egypt, Australia, Japan and Iceland.

Wherever she went, great crowds gathered to see Helen, and famous people, kings, queens and presidents asked to meet her. Many were inspired by her happy, joyful nature.

Annie, though, was often ignored. Helen did not like this – she knew everything she had achieved was thanks to Annie.

Helen and Annie worked hard
for the deaf-blind, demanding
schools and a decent life for them.

Once, in Israel, Helen was told
about a village built especially
for the blind. People expected
her to be pleased, but she was
angry. She said the blind
should not live separately
from everyone else.

Helen had other strong opinions, too. Women could not vote at this time. Campaigners, called suffragettes, wanted to change this.

Chicago Herald

WHY WOMEN
NEED
SUFFRAGE

by Helen Keller

Helen supported them, even when they smashed windows and went on hunger strikes. Many people were shocked. They said a disabled person shouldn't have opinions about the 'real world'.

Disapproval of Helen's views almost stopped a plan to make a film of her life. But it went ahead, and she appeared in it herself. The director gave her instructions by tapping on the floor.

Helen and Annie met many film stars in Hollywood. Charlie Chaplin invited them to his studio.

In 1936, Annie died. She and Helen had been together for almost fifty years. Helen was grief-stricken and missed 'Teacher' terribly for the rest of her life.

But, helped by other assistants, Helen carried on lecturing and touring. She died in 1968, when she was eighty-seven years old.

Helen Keller

Further facts

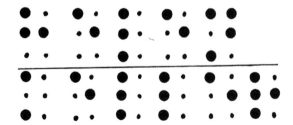

Braille

Braille is named after its inventor,
Louis Braille. At the age of three, he
was blinded in an accident and later
in his life he invented a system of
raised dots representing the letters
of the alphabet. This meant that he
and other blind people could read
using their fingertips.

Telephone inventor

One of the people who advised Helen
Keller's parents on her education,
and later became Helen's great friend,

was Alexander Graham Bell.
His wife was deaf, and
whilst trying to develop
a machine to help the
deaf, Mr Bell invented
the telephone!

Education for the Blind

At the time when Helen Keller was
young, very few blind or deaf-blind
children had the chance of a full
education. Many people thought
children like them could never learn
much or do a useful job. Helen's
great success helped prove these
people wrong.

Some important dates in Helen Keller's lifetime

1880   Helen Keller is born, daughter of Captain Keller and his second wife Kate, in Alabama, USA.

1882   Helen develops a mysterious illness, which leaves her deaf and blind.

1887   Annie Sullivan arrives at the Kellers' home, to work as Helen's teacher.

1900   Helen becomes a student at Radcliffe College.

1902   Helen's first book, 'The Story of My Life', is published.

1918   Helen takes part in a film of her life called 'Deliverance'.

1936   Annie dies. Helen is grief-stricken, but carries on with her work.

1968   Helen dies, aged eighty-seven.